How Are We to Confront Death?

John D. Caputo, *series editor*

PERSPECTIVES IN
CONTINENTAL
PHILOSOPHY

FRANÇOISE DASTUR

How Are We to Confront Death?

An Introduction to Philosophy

Translated by Robert Vallier
Foreword by
David Farrell Krell

FORDHAM UNIVERSITY PRESS
New York ■ 2012

Fordham University Press has no responsibility for the persistence or
accuracy of URLs for external or third-party Internet websites referred
to in this publication and does not guarantee that any content on such
websites is, or will remain, accurate or appropriate.

Fordham University Press also publishes its books in a variety of
electronic formats. Some content that appears in print may not be
available in electronic books.

Library of Congress Cataloging-in-Publication Data is available from the
publisher.

Printed in the United States of America
14 13 12   5 4 3 2 1
First edition

Contents

Foreword

DAVID FARRELL KRELL

Do we ever confront death, either our own or that of others? Do we ever get to see death face-to-face? An ancient wisdom tells us that with regard to our own death there is no confrontation: as long as we live, our death is not there, and when our death is there, we are not alive to confront it. As for the death of others, our culture usually protects us from it: from the basement back door of hospitals to the cemeteries remote from city centers, our entire culture conceals from us the reality of death. It is with death as with that adolescent game played before the mirror, when we try to get at the look of ourselves that would be the look others have of us. We never win at that game, of course: our own gaze chases away the look that others have of us.

Sigmund Freud, in his 1915 "Our Relation to Death," notes that a contradiction or paradox runs through our relation to death. We "know" in some abstract and dispassionate sort of way that we owe a death to nature. We do not need a logic course to demonstrate that if all human beings are mortal, and we ourselves are human beings, then we are going to die. Yet we cannot imagine or represent to ourselves our own death, says Freud, and if there is such a thing as "the unconscious," then its very first precept is the refusal to believe in our own death. For no matter how hard we try to picture it, we ourselves are the observers of whatever it is we picture, and the harder we try, the more obstinately our existence claims the spotlight. Many people in our culture have faith in the immortality of their souls, but it is a far harder and far rarer act of faith to believe that we will die.

Philosophy, from Plato through Schopenhauer, Nietzsche, and Heidegger, is born of the struggle to think about death. The question "How to confront death?" is not just one question among others. Yet it is also right from the start interwoven with questions about love and hate, about what brings folks together and pulls them apart. The death of persons we love cleaves us in two. So much of our unhappiness—and perhaps even our feelings of guilt and blame over the death of others—starts there and stays there, with lovehate and with the passing of persons close to us, no matter how hard our culture tries to shield us. We are scarcely out of kindergarten when we or our little friends lose a grandparent, scarcely out of grade school when a classmate loses a parent or a sibling, scarcely out of high school when we lose one of our own classmates or someone in our own family. We try our best to eat, drink, and be merry, for tomorrow we may have something to think about; our culture meanwhile warns us not to "brood" on death and to live as mindlessly as we can. And it would be lovely if the distractions really worked. Lovely? Maybe not. Some philosophers say that if we are not aware of death, then we cannot be open to anything at all, not even to distractions. It is as though, even if we cannot confront death, it creeps up behind us and overtakes us in any case.

We may be skeptical about that. We may insist that it isn't "healthy" to think about death. It's morbid, in fact. Better to keep on smiling; better to sail on the river of denial. Yet our skepticism and our confident mental hygiene go down the tubes when we fall in love. Falling in love means that someone else's life suddenly becomes very important for our own. It is as though the walls that surround our lonely life begin to crumble, and there we are, exposed to the world outside and to this amazing person. Suddenly the *life* of this astonishing creature is vital to us. And we have to confront, in all our happiness, the worry that this miraculous being is in fact vulnerable. Even if we escape kindergarten, grade school, and high school unscathed, without having to confront death, we would have to escape friendship and love altogether to be really safe. Such safety would not be healthy, however, but really sick. And boring. Deadly dull. So, there we are. And there is death, at least as a menace.

So much about the book you are about to read is wonderful—I won't keep you from it for long, but will just point out a few things in it that strike me as particularly fine. Françoise Dastur, who is one of the leading lights in contemporary French philosophy, begins with the dilemma or paradox sketched above, and she doesn't try to reduce the difficulty of confrontation with death. She respects the difficulty, as she respects her reader. She places demands on us. The first demand, in her discussion of "overcoming death," is to steer a middle course between traditional beliefs in the immortality of the soul and the modern scientistic view that scoffs at all such beliefs. Dastur argues that human beings need to sustain some sort of relation to the dead, so that belief in immortality is not merely an illusion that has to be squelched. And yet there is no doubt that the sciences—both the natural sciences and the cultural sciences—have put in question every traditional religious cult or belief about death and immortality. Neither blind faith nor scoffing will do. Rather, it is a matter of recognizing that our modern propensity to get rid of our dead as quickly as possible so that we can get back to work without any further inconvenience may not be so "scientific" after all. And it is also a matter of recognizing that the feeling of emptiness and frustration that we have with most of our traditional ways of dealing with death is quite justified. Where death is concerned, illusions do abound. How to avoid an attitude of disdain, then, but also evade the most vulgar forms of delusion? No one who goes to confront the question of death nowadays can escape from this double task, the need neither to mock nor to embrace illusions. Instead, Dastur argues that we need to learn *how to question* with persistence and patience.

These are exciting times for the biological sciences, and the progress of technology in the medical and biological realms is more than impressive. Yet even the theory of the immortality of germ cells does not eliminate the reality of sepsis, exhaustion, and death at the heart of life processes. Entropy seems to operate not only in the universe of physics, but also at the core of somatic cellular life. Yet these are also exciting times for a philosophy of life and the environment: neither "life" nor "death" seem to be adequate concepts nowadays, and some recent philosophers have even risked writing the word *lifedeath*. The contradiction would be not merely conceptual, but truly existential. As Dastur argues, however, amortality—the confidence that organic life will some day be able to go on and on without confronting a limit—is probably more dubious than any notion of immortality. Our pop culture loves cyborgs and robots and intelligence-inducing monoliths because these fulfill the need for comforting illusions. The sciences themselves, in spite of their public-relations propaganda, have become more cautious. It turns out that Sophocles is not out of date when he has his chorus chant, in *Antigone*, that whereas human beings have discovered astonishing cures for diseases of all kinds, the cure for death continues to elude them.

If death cannot be overcome in any straightforward way, can we at least "neutralize" it by parrying the blow of the anxiety it induces? Among the strategies we employ, Dastur, like the Diotima of Plato's *Symposium*, emphasizes human reproduction and the transmission of works that we hand down to tradition. And, again like Diotima, she gives the transmission of works, especially the works of written language, precedence over genetic transmission. If such emphasis is by now quite familiar to us—Shakespeare makes it over and over again in his sonnets, promising that his inky lines will last longer than his ageing body and his frustrated loves—it may be because literature, music, and the arts have not relinquished their power as a stratagem, if not to foil death, then at least to resist the total oblivion that death seems to have in store for us. Throughout her little book, Dastur argues for the importance of a diachronic relation of the generations: to be fully human is to be in some way connected to one's forebears and to one's successors on the stage of life. Such a vertical connection among generations is difficult for U.S.-Americans to understand, since our culture celebrates youth and scorns old age. Short-term memory, not long-term, is our strength, and oblivion is where we spend most of our time. "Fully human" is perhaps an expression that embarrasses us, especially if it commits us to who or what has gone before and will come after us. If we take great pride in our oblivion, as we do generally in our capacity for stupefaction, this call to think fore and aft will strike us as strange. Maybe even impossible.

What will *not* strike us as strange is Dastur's analysis of those familiar ways in which our culture tries to neutralize anxiety through the cult of the body, behaviors that expose us to the thrill of extreme risk, and the craving for celebrity. We attack and scar our bodies, we pop pills and rush into surgeries in order to show that our bodies belong to us, that we are their masters, that we would never permit anything like death to demonstrate to us our ineluctable passivity. We bungee jump, we leap howling from airplanes, we pay great sums to scale Everest, we go to every length to be in the limelight, be in the movies, we sacrifice everything to keep the spotlight fixed on us—not because we affirm who and what we are, but in order to flee our mortal condition. We pretend to be gods and goddesses in the hope that if the others are sufficiently fooled by us, they will help us to fool ourselves. Although these behaviors seem to ally themselves with the body and to spurn the soul, they beat both body and soul alike into submission, as though in this way to get the better of death. And virtual reality? It is perhaps the best way to hide one's body and soul from others. We are all atwitter in splendid isolation, and we prefer Facebook to faces. We walk down Fifth Avenue and see everyone absorbed in telephone conversations, talking away to an invisible ear, rambling on and on as though they are all completely nuts, *Enheslike, I'm just crossing Forty-Second Street right now and there's a bus full of tourists, enumlike I toadily couldn't care less where you are, tourists from where? enheslike Dunno, but they've all got cameras hey maybe I'll be in all their home movies! enumlike Say cheese etc. etc. etc.*, gabbing to no one in particular, everyone hiding out, everyone tele-blabbing, everyone avoiding eye contact with everyone else like the plague and concealing their forsakenness by engaging in the technological autism that marks our social world. It seems to work, seems to hold death at bay. Virtually.

Yet the entire force of Dastur's book is to get us to stop "overcoming," stop "neutralizing," and to "accept" death, accepting it as a kind of responsibility that, admittedly, is too big for me, taking up the possibility of my own death as a burden or task. Here it is clear that arguments and logical propositions won't help us. Indeed, everything here is debatable, or, rather, a matter for serious and patient discussion. (One of the places where I cannot follow Dastur, for example, is her treatment of suicide—which I do not at all take to be a "dodging" of death; I look forward to having the chance to talk the matter over with her, to listen and reconsider, confident that she will be doing the same.) To accept our death means to affirm our mortality. It means to refuse to run away from the reality of death, or at least to face up to it from time to time, to let my life be informed by this important crossroads, to realize (without brooding over it) that the crossroads is not out there at a distance, but right here with me at each step of my life. My being-toward-the-end does not rule my life at every instant, but it is there as a kind of constant. It doesn't "ground" my life, because death is an abyss, not a ground. Yet the abyss is a fundamental feature of my landscape, and I can't afford to ignore it. Besides, I've lost family and friends to death, and wanting to stay close to them, I have to think about this strange affair of our living and dying. I have to own up to it. Not overcome it, not neutralize it, but in some way to accept it.

The final pages of Dastur's book are the most challenging and the most exciting of all. Her account of the role of death in Christian religious traditions, in Plato's dialogue

Phaedo, and in the *Essays* of Michel de Montaigne is succinct and judicious. Dastur herself would not take it amiss if I were to suggest that other religious traditions need to be considered here, not only the great world religions of Hinduism, Judaism, and Islam, and but also the sundry Buddhist schools; each of these religions and life practices has something quite particular to say about death in life and life in death. And it might also be worthwhile to distinguish the attitudes toward death in the various Christian sects themselves, from the fundamentalist varieties of the U.S. of A. to the Protestantisms of Northern Europe and the Catholicisms of Southern Europe, as well as the Orthodox traditions of Eastern Europe. (I recall an Italian philosopher explaining to me why there are so many nativity scenes in Italian art: "We like mothers and babies," she said, "and we don't like all that blood.") Such considerations would be just the beginning, for surely every people and every culture and not a few animals in each nook and cranny of the Earth have something in their way of confronting death that would astonish us and make us think. Dastur's pages here are merely a start, I'm sure she'd agree.

That said, it would be more controversial to say, as I would say, that something revolutionary happens to our thinking about death when we read the prologue to Friedrich Nietzsche's *Thus Spoke Zarathustra*. There, Nietzsche recounts Zarathustra's teaching of the "Overman," which is not a "Superman" (Nietzsche hasn't been reading the comics), but a kind of human being who crosses over to a new kind of humanity by embracing wholeheartedly the mortal condition: to go across or to cross over toward this new affirmation of mortality, says Zarathustra, is to acknowledge that one must go under, one must go down. Don't bury your head in the sands of heavenly dreams, he will later say, but let your dying be an act of fidelity to the

Earth. Such terrestrial fidelity has an impact on the way Zarathustra treats other people, and Nietzsche dramatizes this in his account (in the prologue) of the tightrope walker.

The townspeople are gathered at the market place; all gaze upward at the man on wire. Horribly, however, the tightrope walker loses his balance at midwire when a clown outperforms him by leaping over him. The clown causes the one who crosses over to plummet to the pavement below. He lands at the very spot where Zarathustra happens to be standing.

> But Zarathustra remained right where he was. The body landed next to him, horribly fractured, horribly mangled, but not yet dead. After a while, the shattered man regained consciousness; he saw Zarathustra kneeling beside him. "What are you doing here?" he said finally. "I've long known the devil would trip me up. And now he's going to drag me off to hell. Would you try to stop him?"
>
> "By my honor, friend," answered Zarathustra, "there is no devil and no hell. Your soul will be dead before your body: you have nothing more to fear!"
>
> The man looked up, full of mistrust. He then said, "If you are telling the truth, then I lose nothing when I lose my life. I'm not much more than an animal that's been taught to dance by those who beat him and toss him little treats."
>
> "Not so," said Zarathustra. "You have made danger your vocation, and there is nothing contemptible about that. Now your vocation has laid you low. For that reason I will bury you with my own hands."
>
> After Zarathustra had said these words, the dying man replied no more. Yet he moved his hand, as though searching for the hand of Zarathustra, in order to thank him.—[1]

Not even Montaigne dared to say, and to mean it as a comforting thought, "Your soul will be dead before your body." This is the thought that young Simmias and Cebes had as they were talking with Socrates in his cell during the final moments of the great man's life, the moments depicted so tellingly in Plato's *Phaedo*. Yet all the young men present were visibly crushed by the thought, so that Simmias and Cebes scarcely dared to utter it. A millennium or two had to pass before Nietzsche found the courage to say it aloud and think it through.

Heidegger, of course, read Nietzsche pretty carefully. And it is to Heidegger's *Being and Time* of 1927 that Françoise Dastur guides us in the final pages of her book. Albert Camus, when he read *Being and Time*, confessed his astonishment:

> Heidegger coolly considers the human condition and announces that our existence is humiliated. . . . This professor of philosophy writes without trembling and in the most abstract language imaginable that "the finite and limited character of human existence is more primordial than the human being himself" [*Kant and the Problem of Metaphysics*, section 41]. For him it is no longer necessary to doze; indeed, he must remain awake up to the very consummation. He persists in this absurd world; he stresses its perishability. He gropes his way amid ruins.[2]

Among the words that seemed to Camus so abstract, so cold, are those that Heidegger uses to define a new confrontation with death, the confrontation he calls "existential." Death is in each case my own; indeed, it is what is *most my own, my ownmost* possibility. Death is *nonrelational*, in the sense that I cannot find a representative who will stand in for me and take it off my back and out of my future; someone may rescue me from danger, but both she and I will not be able in the end to pass our dying onto someone else. Furthermore, death cannot be *overtaken*, we cannot get around it, surpass it, or pass it by; death is *impassible*, though certainly not impossible. In fact, death is precisely *the possibility that is most my own, nonrelational, and impassible*. Finally, and most paradoxically, death is the possibility of our existence that is *most certain*, not as an item of knowledge or as a conviction, but *certain* precisely in the *indeterminability of its "when."* As for immortality, says Heidegger, perhaps a bit wryly, we'll talk about it when we get there. For the moment, what human existence needs to focus on, in spite of all the distractions to which it falls prey, is its being toward the end, its being toward death.[3]

It is important that I remember here at the end of these introductory remarks something that I ought to have noted at the outset. The book's title has a question mark at the end. Dastur's is not a "how-to" book. It won't *tell* us how we are to confront death; it only *asks* how we may do so. Dastur wants to avoid every willful sort of answer, because our finitude—our very nature as heading toward the end—cannot be overcome by an exercise of will. We were raised to think that where there's a will, there's a way, but we knew when we heard this expression, over and over again, that when it comes to the important things in life, it's a really dumb thing to say. And our dying is one of the important things. Dastur is by no means sure that we *can* confront death, but she is convinced—and she convinces me—that we have to *try*, even if trying has nothing to do with willpower. It has rather to do with developing the capacity to let be, to release matters from our grasp, and to detach ourselves from our tendency to push and pull, pull and push, until the objects of our desire capitulate. In Dastur's view, we have to learn how to think within anxiety, giving up the dream that the horror and the anxiety that death arouses in us will be laid to rest by some magical incantation, giving up the hope that we may be superheroes who freeze or burn or clobber or otherwise discombobulate the death toward which our life is moving. Today, when everything is dominated by the will to plan, control, and master through technology every aspect of our lives, the thinking that lets be will strike us as unprecedented. So it is, unless in certain Eastern philosophies and in Meister Eckhart. Much would change if we could learn this new way of thinking, thinking within anxiety, but also with detachment and a talent for letting be.

Among the things that would change would be the doctor-patient relation. Physicians would no longer be master mechanics, nor would they be the high priests of life and death. Rather, they would work in partnership with their patients, laboring on the side of life, as always, but not to the point where life loses all its vitality and all its dignity. A generation ago, the behaviorists urged us to move beyond freedom and dignity, to get over them. Dastur demurs. Palliative medicine supports the patient's desire to live, and to live well, but it will not promise to postpone death indefinitely, will not support our spending our final days as vegetables hooked up to machines, crock pots for people.

There is hardly an aspect of our lives that would not be altered by a thoughtful confrontation with death. To think about life and death is to engage in a kind of action that, while relatively quiet and fairly discreet, has the power to change everything. At the end of her book, Dastur writes: "*Becoming* a mortal would require that we stop giving in to the illusions of immortality and become capable of truly living on the earth and dwelling in a body." Becoming a mortal would enable us to see death, not as an imperfection, but as an essential capacity of the human being. Such think-ing would never overcome anxiety. Rather, it would learn to dwell in anxiety. Yet thinking within anxiety would also be, as Dastur says, "in no way incompatible with the joy of existing."

David Farrell Krell
DePaul University

How Are We to Confront Death?

Introduction

How do we confront death? This question seems to impose itself in a particularly insistent manner at certain critical moments, such as when our life is in danger, but in reality, it never goes away and always more or less obviously accompanies us throughout our existence. The human being is that strange animal that *knows* that it must one day die. Nobody doubts that the feeling of a fundamental vulnerability is commonly shared by all living beings. But the human being is the only being that is aware of the ephemeral character of its existence. It knows that its existence cannot be indefinitely extended and that just as it had to begin, so, too, one day it will have to end. Birth and death, those two apparently extreme limits of existence, are events that happen in the world only to others, not to those who actually undergo them and thus have no control over them. We can certainly accelerate or delay death, we can provoke it by suicide or prolong it with the appropriate care—but we cannot choose whether or not to die, just as we cannot choose whether or not to be born. And just as I was not contemporaneous with my own birth—which I did not want and which represents a past that is in some way absolute, a past that was never present for me and that therefore I cannot remember—so, too, is my death a future event that will never happen to me, since I will no longer be there to witness it, even though I know I cannot escape it. And if something about our own birth remains incomprehensible for each of us (since, for example, the possibility of not having come into the world seems unimaginable), our reason is all the more disarmed by death, that enigma of the total disappearance of our own being. Birth and death are therefore not events marking out the external limits of an existence, but are rather fundamental dimensions of existing. And just as each individual will have to take on the determinations inherited merely by being born, so, too, must each individual confront the perspective of his own death yet to come [à venir].

But if it is already impossible for us to imagine a world where we would not exist, how, then, could we ever represent our own death to ourselves? We know that this is what led Freud to claim that "at bottom no one believes in his own death, or, to put the same thing in another way, that in the unconscious every one of us is convinced of his own immortality."[1] We will never meet death in person, even though we never stop feeling its invisible presence weighing on us, and as soon as we try to think it, we make it into an event in the world, even though it is nothing but the pure and simple disappearance of whoever undergoes it. There is thus no experience of death as such: this is what led Epicurus to claim that "death is of no concern to us, for while we exist death is not present, and where death is present, we no longer exist."[2] The death with which we are instead confronted is always the death of others, and in particular of those who are close to us. The foremost experience is, for us, the experience of mourning. But the death of the other also hurts us because it awakens in us the latent consciousness of our own mortality that constitutes the hidden face of our existence. For the human becomes aware of itself as human only through anxiety in the face of death, which is what is brought back to life by the death of the other.

We thus have access to our humanity only through an awareness of our own mortality and through our experience of anxiety. Death is an object of horror for everyone, and it seems that we are able to confront it in thought only insofar as we are able to relativize it. There is apparently no possible human existence without this struggle against death, and in this regard, we can view the whole of humanity's cultural productions as a variety of defense mechanisms or barriers erected against death and as arms destined to keep it at bay. Such a struggle is in vain, however, because we all know death always wins in the end. But there are different ways to lead the combat. We could either imagine ourselves as capable of vanquishing the adversary and as able to give ourselves the means to counter it: *overcoming death* is thus a task that human being gives itself, and this task is also at the origin of the rise of religions and the sciences. Or, faced with the anxiety generated by the very idea of death, we could try to outwit it and find ways of *neutralizing death* through an ensemble of behaviors that seem to make it retreat.

But is death really the enemy? Does confronting it necessarily mean combating it or to trying to escape it? Does not the human being have the possibility of *accepting death* and of consenting to it,[3] which would not be recognizing defeat, but would instead consist in seeing in death the very condition of life and in considering mortality less as a limit than as the secret resource nourishing existence?

Overcoming Death

The Immortality of the Soul and the Practices of Mourning

Though most animals disregard the corpses of their dead, humans have buried their dead since time immemorial. We could thus rightly consider that the practice of funeral rites, more than the use of tools or the invention of language, is what characterizes the very advent of human being. These rites are not limited simply and solely to inhumation and burial, but also include mummification, cremation, and even the exposing of the dead, which is not merely the abandonment of the corpse to the work of nature, since in the rare cultures that have adopted it, this work is likewise surrounded by a complex ritual.[1] Such practices mark the advent of the reign of culture, because they testify to a refusal to submit to the natural order, the cycle of life and death that rules over all living creatures. The refusal is surely only a symbolic gesture, since it is not possible to oppose the irreversible, but the gesture nevertheless testifies to human beings' ambiguous relation with death, a relation that is both a recognition and a denial: a recognition, because the funeral rite is a way of taking note of the death of the dearly departed, the deceased,[2] who has come to the end of his or her existence, but also a denial, because a new mode of relation with the one who has passed away, but who now continues to exist in the great beyond, is accessed through the rite itself.[3]

Thanks to the work of anthropologists, today we know that even in archaic societies, humans refused to consider death as a total disappearance and continued to maintain relations with the invisible world of the dead. We therefore cannot view the invention of "the beyond" simply as a fact of established religions. The idea of a life after death obviously takes on different forms, depending on how it is conceived: in the case of ancient Greece, it was conceived as a spectral living on, as a diminished form of life, whereas theories of reincarnation, in contrast, teach a rebirth and the passage to a new form of life. Christianity's novel contribution (which in fact had a precedent in Mazdeism)[4] is not only the idea of a linear (and no longer cyclical) temporality, but also the idea of a "last judgment" and of the "resurrection of the body." The world of the here and now is definitively cut off from the world beyond, and "the beyond" no longer refers merely to a life prolonged beyond death, but instead to an "eternal life," an idea that is decisively triumphant.

This notion of a veritable "beyond" of earthly life is central to Christianity, but also emphatically has been called into question, beginning with the Enlightenment, which can be characterized both as a struggle against obscurantism and as the rise of an atheism for which certain nineteenth-century philosophers are the spokesmen. This was particularly the case for Karl Marx. As we know, he viewed this belief in a "beyond" as the fundamental form of human alienation, denouncing it as the "opiate of the people."[5] This was also the case for Friedrich Nietzsche, for whom the invention of this "afterworld," which is the world of the beyond, is the hidden source of modern nihilism.[6] But the belief that death is not the final end for everything nonetheless still remains deeply entrenched and compelling, even among nonbelievers. We must try to understand what constitutes the deep-seated motivation of this belief, and an examination of the practices of mourning can be instructive for this purpose.

All funeral rites are concerned with overcoming the horror aroused by the sight of the corpse of the departed. And the cadaver is indeed disturbing, not only because it is decaying and is the source of pollution, but also because it occupies a strange intermediary place between the inert thing and the living person. The cadaver is therefore an object of anxiety and terror, and it must be set apart if we are to establish the possibility of renewing the relationship with the deceased, which was brutally interrupted by death. This is what takes place through the intermediary of the funeral rite, allowing for the establishment of a uniquely spiritual link with the deceased, who then in some way remains "with" the living. Disposing of the corpse in order to allow for the reestablishment of a virtual relation with the deceased is the profound meaning of funeral rites. A human being does not live in community only with his or her contemporaries, but also, and perhaps above all, with those who have preceded him or her in time. This community of life with the spirits of ancestors constitutes the unitary foundation of all cultures and is what serves as the basis of the fundamental phenomenon of transmission and thus, tradition.

The mission or purpose of funeral rites is to guarantee that the individual who has just died does not completely disappear, that something of the individual remains and endures, at least in the memory of the survivors; it is this invisible presence of the departed that was first called "soul." This is not simply an irrational belief, but what corresponds to the experience that each person may have of herself as soon as she tries to represent her own death to herself. I can easily imagine a world where I, as an empirical individual made up of an intertwining of multiple factual determinations, no longer am. I share with other humans these factual determinations (sex, ethnicity, particular physical traits, date and place of birth, etc.), and only their particular arrangement in me is what truly singularizes me. What seems to resist death is the field of anonymous consciousness that I also am and without which no world could ever appear. An unconditioned self emerges from the disappearance or death of the empirical ego, a self that does not itself undergo death and that thereby constitutes the true foundation of the belief in the immortality of the soul. Just as the chapter of the *Upanishads* celebrates (about five hundred years before the birth of Jesus) the supratemporality or even nontemporality of the *Atman*, the absolute self, so, too, does Plato, in the *Phaedo* (about one hundred years after the *Upanishads*) bet on the immortality of the soul—as will German philosophy from Kant to Husserl, in which a transcendental ego that can neither be born nor die is opposed to the empirical ego, which alone is mortal.

Whether it is obvious or not, what is therefore celebrated in every funeral ritual is what in the human transgresses the limited share of life granted to the individual. But, one will ask, what is it about the modern era, at least in the West, that leads not only to an increasing decline in the belief in the existence of a beyond and in the immortality of the soul, but that also makes death itself so insignificant that the public practices of mourning seem to be reduced to their most minimal expression? It is specifically in our epoch—when historical and anthropological knowledge have more than ever before allowed us to be aware of the central role that the relation to death plays in the constitution of the humanity of the human—and in our modern societies that we bear witness to a demystification of death, to what we will call, as Hans-Georg Gadamer does, a real "repression of death."[7] Such a repression arises from the technical consequences of the Industrial Revolution in the West and from the changes they have wrought in the lives of humans. In this respect, we must underline the fact that increasing urbanization has made a number of funeral practices obsolete, including the mortuary cortege, the gathering of the family and friends around the body of the dead. And we must also emphasize that the disappearance of the public representation of death goes together with the increasing distancing of the dying from his or her place of origin.

In the last decades of the twentieth century, then, we could rightly say not only that death has constituted the principal interdiction or taboo of modernity (just as sex once did),[8] but also that contemporary society favors the attitude of flight from death, thus engendering a denial of death, as expressed by the fact that we no longer find the time or space to integrate the dying and the dead.[9] But at the same time, one of the consequences of increasing individualism has been to reinforce fantasies of personal immortality, which might lead us to believe that this "deritualization of mourning" to which we today bear witness in fact arises from a new and more intimate way of conceiving death and of living mourning.[10]

The whole question, however, is to know whether these new and more intimate practices also give survivors the possibility of "overcoming" death, which means maintaining an ambiguous relation with death, consisting somewhat dialectically in observing death while also denying it. But what is happening today is not a kind of "sublation" of or "relief" from death through the belief in an immortality of the soul, but rather a psychologization of mourning. Funerals have been profoundly modified: instead of obeying an ostentatious protocol, they now require the personal engagement of close friends in the ceremony. During the ceremony, the personality of the deceased is evoked, the circumstances of his or her death and the noteworthy events of his or her life are recalled, the deceased is even sometimes addressed as if he or she were still present, and texts are read or bits of music are played for the deceased. Once a fundamental social demonstration, mourning has now become a psychological effort for neutralizing death.

Edgar Morin, who was among the first anthropologists to be interested in the relation that humans have with death, claims that the long repression to which the question of death has been subjected in the West seems today to have come to an end.[11] But we can legitimately wonder if this "return to death" at work in what we might call the "privatization" of mourning can indeed open out onto something other than an "impossible mourning."[12] Thanks to these new "preneed funeral contracts," dying persons now have the possibility of organizing their own funerals, which certainly amounts to "personalizing" them, but also to taking away the responsibility for them from survivors. Mourners are imperatively called upon to "be in mourning," which means in other words to "manage" it in the most effective manner possible, as if it were a matter of immediately sealing off the painful breach opened by the other's death. For the same reason, we summon as reinforcements for the families of the victims of catastrophes cohorts of psychologists and grief counselors, armies of antibodies delegated by the social organism who are supposed to help families begin their "work" of mourning without delay. But is mourning really a matter of "work," a task to be executed, or is it on the contrary a process that we should be *let happen* by itself?[13] The whole process happens as if it were obeying the modern social imperative of "breaking even" or "profitability" and of getting rid of the dead as quickly as possible. This is why mourning must be managed in the least visible manner possible, without disturbing the social environment of the grieving. We must in some way "be done" with death, erase every trace of the deceased, which perhaps explains why we make ever-increasing recourse to cremation,[14] reducing the place made for the dead as much as possible and taking the dead out of public space.

It is only too obvious that such a practice of mourning will only fail to produce what it intends: instead of a process allowing for the establishment of a spiritual relation with the departed, the loss of whom is thereby *publicly* attested, "privatized mourning" can result only in a spectral incorporation of the deceased, who then remains as a strange body that continues to haunt the soul of the grieving.[15] Making a place for the dead in the generational chain is what allowed ancient funeral rites to be centered on the dead themselves, rather than on the survivors, which is now the case when we try to expel the dead from memory by ordering the grieving to "do" their mourning.

Belief in the immortality of the soul, we've seen, is not simply a metaphysical hypothesis or an ideological superstructure that must be undone at any price in an "enlightened" modernity. In reality, it fulfills an essential function, serving as a basis for the exchange between the living and the dead without which no human existence is possible. Yet today we are witnessing a true change of perspective in the understanding that human being has of itself, insofar as it tends to submit to one single scientific discourse in accounting for its experience and insofar as this discourse has acquired an exclusive preponderance in relation to every other kind of discourse, including the religious and the philosophical. These latter, though still and always present, have nonetheless lost their authority. Fundamental human phenomena such as birth, sickness, and death, and indeed human being itself, have been unconditionally submitted to the authority of the natural sciences. As a consequence, these phenomena now appear to be "objective" processes, exterior and contingently happening to a human being. It is in this way that death itself ceases to appear as an indisputable factual given.

The Amortality of the Body and the Promises of Modern Science

Because human being is unable to accept the finitude of its earthly condition, the idea of the soul was invented. But what follows from this "invention" is the division of the human into two parts: the immortal soul, which is akin to the divine, and the body, which belongs to the order of becoming, the order of what is born and dies. From this follows the idea that we find in ancient Greece, in Orphic myths, and in Plato—the idea of the *somasema*, the body tomb,[16] by which the divine part of the human being is imprisoned in the earthly part prior to being freed by various practices.

This distinction between the body and the soul—which seems so obvious to us, since distinct sciences such as biology and psychology deal with them today, despite the expansion of the neurosciences—is in fact not at all obvious. We ought not be surprised to see this distinction vigorously contested, starting from the moment that belief in the beyond begins to decline. Friedrich Nietzsche is probably the most notable representative in modern philosophy of this will to reverse the hierarchy established between body and soul: in "the highest functions of the spirit" he finds "only sublimated organic functions."[17] For him, the hypothesis of the soul is thus entirely possible, but always and only on the condition of truly breaking with the dualist conception that we usually have of human being; this would imply no longer reducing the body to a machine, to the body as the object of science, but instead seeing in it the true subject of thought. This is what allows Nietzsche to put the body in the place previously occupied by the soul and to claim in contrast that "the logic of our conscious thought" is only a "crude and simplified form of that thought, which our organism, and even more, each of its various organs, needs."[18] However, this rehabilitation of the body inaugurated by Nietzsche and continuously developed in contemporary thought is not yet an affirmation of its "amortality," that is, of its aptitude to live indefinitely. In this regard, and even though Nietzsche, like Spinoza, considers that true "wisdom is a meditation on life, not on death,"[19] he has not yet broken with the ancient idea according to which we humans can do nothing about death. In an oft-cited passage from Sophocles' tragedy *Antigone*, the chorus, praising human being, defines it as the greatest marvel, yet also as the most disturbing being, for it is only by violating the natural order that it is able to establish the human reign of the *polis*, or city-state. Humans must recognize that they can do nothing against death, which escapes all of their ruses.[20]

Hans Jonas, citing the chorus in his *Imperative of Responsibility*, sees in it a testament to a conception of human technology wholly different from the one characterizing our era. Until the beginning of the modern age, the sole purpose of human technology was to make the lives of humans easier, and the human city was constituted only as a limited enclave within nature, whose omnipotence remained unchallenged. The situation is now completely different. Human action has not only extended its domain of action, but has also qualitatively changed its nature. The experimental or scientific method, which imposed itself in the seventeenth century with Cartesianism, has radically transformed the scientific ideal, because the practical application of knowledge is now a part of science itself. It seems today that technological progress in itself constitutes humanity's only purpose, as if the vocation of humanity were to arrive at the complete and total domination of the world. The very existence of the world is no longer independent of human action, and the whole of nature is thus subjected to (or subjugated by) technological action, which some decades ago had the consequence of bringing to birth a new science of the environment: ecology. The frontier between the natural and the human worlds thus tends to become abolished, while actual technology has become a new sort of nature. Jonas begins with the idea that the promise of modern technology—that of a better and more livable world for humankind—is inverted into a threat and that this menace has not only the physical meaning of the possible destruction of the entire planet in the atomic age, but also the moral meaning of the destruction of the humanity of the human. Jonas concludes from this that what subsequently enters into the sphere of human responsibility is

Overcoming Death ■ *13*

nothing short of the entire biosphere itself. But there's more: human being has itself become an object of technology, and not merely the subject of technical action. In being able to apply to itself its own technical prowess, humans have in some ways elevated technology above nature.

We know today that human behavior can be biochemically controlled. And to this possibility of the social manipulation and programming of individuals to the detriment of their individual autonomy is added another, still more disturbing possibility—genetic manipulation, which allows humans to take charge of their own genetic evolution. Humans have also seen their own mortality change meaning: death, which seemed to elicit what in the human condition is unchangeable, now "no longer appears as a necessity belonging to the nature of life, but as an avoidable, at least in principle tractable and long-delayable organic malfunction."[21] From this follows what Jonas calls the "utopian" character of technological progress, which pushes us toward goals that previously seemed out of reach.

There is progress in the sciences, and in particular in cellular biology, that holds out the possibility of reversing the aging process and of indefinitely extending human life. The body, traditionally conceived as the site of aging and of death, now acquires a new status, the status of *amortality*, since the cells that form it seem potentially immortal. The classical opposition of life and death and the validity of Bichat's abundantly cited formula stating that "life consists in the sum of the functions by which death is resisted" are thus now called into question.[22] In the perspective of the famous late eighteenth-century French physiologist, which is to say, in the vitalist perspective, life is defined as a force that defies physical laws. Because it is in the nature of vital properties to exhaust themselves, however, death is the ineluctable destiny of the living being, which finally succumbs to the aggression of external forces. But in contrast,

August Weismann, the German biologist from the second half of the nineteenth century who, in the unanimous opinion of specialists, is at the origin of the progress of current biology, claims that "death, that is, the end of life, is by no means, as is usually assumed, an essential attribute of all organisms."[23] Weismann distinguishes two kinds of cells— "germinal" cells, which are directly implicated in the reproduction of the organism, and "somatic" cells. Only the first kind is virtually immortal, in that these cells can be transmitted to and transformed into a new organism. What this kind of immortality of the germinal lineage therefore assures is the integrity of the species and the continuity of life. This is what will form the basis of modern genetics and its key concept of the "genetic program," that is, of hereditary memory. But if there is indeed something immortal transmitted through us, this does not in any way mean that we ourselves participate as individuals in such immortality, because once the hereditary characteristics have been transmitted, the individual is nothing more than an "accessory appendage," which death cannot but claim, given that its somatic cells possess only a limited capacity of renewal.

Far from having a substantial permanence, our body is on the contrary constantly becoming: the majority of cells of which it is composed have highly variable life expectancies ranging from a few days to a few weeks. The apparent continuity of life is thus in reality made up of a multitude of discontinuities. And so in a way, we come back to La-marck's intuition that death is inscribed in the very heart of the living being.[24] We thus end up with a new notion of life, no longer understood as a positive phenomenon, but instead as what results from the repression of self-destruction, and with a new conception of death, because "a radically new image of death as a sculptor at the heart of the living is, at least at the cellular level, superimposed on the ancient image of death as the Grim Reaper arriving from the outside to destroy."[25] We are at every moment in the midst of dying and of being reborn; maintaining ourselves in life depends on the equilibrium established in us between the forces of destruction and the forces of renewal. This new, dynamic, and plastic vision of the organism should allow us to become aware, already just on the biological level, of the indissociability of life and death in us.

The vision that life can be indefinitely repeated and can endure has also been thrown out of favor by the progress of contemporary physics.[26] We know that since the famous second law of thermodynamics was formulated in the nineteenth century, stipulating that an increase in entropy is inevitable, the hypothesis of a universal degradation and of an eventual thermal death of the universe has been envisioned. This hypothesis has only been strengthened by recent discoveries in astrophysics. Astronomers are now capable not only of predicting that in about six billion years our sun will enter into the final phase of its life, but also of determining that at twelve billion years of age, our galaxy is already quite old and has practically exhausted its resources. Scientists also predict that the hundreds of billions of other galaxies populating the universe will likely undergo the same evolution. The theory of the expanding universe formulated by Hubble in 1929 and the theory of the Big Bang that the majority of physicists today support are not at all in contradiction with the hypothesis of the slow degradation of the universe, of its finally sinking into a giant black hole that itself will also probably come to an end by evaporating. Though predictions of modern cosmology have shown that the future of the universe extends much further than imagined in the nineteenth century, it seems that we nevertheless end up at the same conclusion—the inexorable death of the universe.

Attempts to overcome death through mythical stories, religious beliefs, metaphysical hypotheses, and scientific utopias have been pursued since the birth of humanity, but none are able to quell the anxiety that humans feel when faced with the prospect of our own annihilation. And yet, unable to look death in the face, humans may still try to neutralize death through a variety of ruses.

2

Neutralizing Death

Are we not totally disarmed by the anxiety that grips us at the thought of our own death? Humans are not alone in knowing fear, the feeling of vulnerability piercing the very heart of all living beings. But the feeling of anxiety— this emotion that, as its name clearly implies,[1] grabs us by throat, cuts off our speech, and brutally tears us from the familiarity of our daily environment—is proper to human being. An extreme experience of radical forsakenness, anxiety places the human being directly in front of the nothingness that is its lot, thereby revealing the most extreme possibility, the collapse of all possibilities that is death.[2]

In a manner sometimes marked with Pascalian accents, Heidegger extensively analyzed the ruses that humans deploy to hide their own mortality from themselves and all the "diversions" that they invent to forget about it.[3] How can we not see in the frenzied action motivating so many of our contemporaries a pathetic flight from what ineluctably awaits them, an expiration that they obscurely hope to delay? For them, death has the face of an event yet to come from which they are still separated by an indefinite number of days, an event that they must parry[4] at any price. When faced with such an ungraspable enemy, it seems necessary to elaborate a whole strategy.

Reproduction and Transmission

If a singular being can neither acquire immortality for itself nor extend its life indefinitely, it might instead somehow procure these through transmitting its genes or its name. By thus giving itself a future that goes beyond the limits of its own existence, humans can have the delusion of keeping death at a distance. We must not underestimate the power in human being of this will to survive beyond itself in its descendents or in its works, and we have to recognize that this power is no doubt what more or less consciously animates humans and motivates a number of their actions. We find here in this general human strategy of transmission the two different paths—of the body and of the mind—that the human takes in the efforts that it unfurls to overcome death.

The transmitting of genes occurs in different living beings, but because it is not in any way a matter of a conscious will, we will have to give up the originally anthropomorphic idea that nature pursues some end or other. The Greeks named this blind push toward the visible *physis*, a word with the same root as *phos*, which means "light." We must not be in a rush to claim that death has the utility of permitting the regeneration and survival of the species. The idea that death would be the "obligatory ransom of sexuality" is seductive,[5] because it not only lets us think that there is an intrinsic link between death and individuation, but also lets us give at least a biological meaning to death. But as the most recent studies show, there is no necessary relation between sexuality and death, nor a natural law that would inexorably condemn every living being to aging and death.[6] Nor is there any "resurrection by sex"[7] that would be, so to speak, inscribed in the program of nature or that could constitute an imperative that all living beings, including human beings, would unknowingly obey.

It is true that things are presented differently in human societies, where there is a concern for the preservation of the species and a valuing of reproductive activity, which explains the importance of the institutions and rites attached to it in all cultures. It is nevertheless the case that human being most often continues to be conceived according to a strictly biological model. We know that in certain living species, death brutally follows after reproduction. An individual in the animal world dies as soon as it attains the plenitude of its purpose, as if an extension of its life would have no utility. It is entirely different with humans, who do not necessarily consider the act of reproduction to be the goal of existence and who often have the feeling that they are fated to die before having exhausted all the possibilities of their being. A human being consequently has the tendency to judge that no matter how long its existence may be, it is nevertheless always too brief and death always premature. This feeling of the brevity of life pushes humans to transmit their knowledge to subsequent generations, and this phenomenon of transmission is at the origin of culture and history: descendents of the deceased can take up again and bring to completion the projects that the deceased did not have the time to complete.

The human being, like other living beings, can live on only through its descendants. But there is "reproduction" in the strict sense of the term only in nature, where the same cycle of life is repeated from genitor to progenitor. It is not the same for the human being, who has the possibility of giving its own existence an entirely new form. We can therefore say that in human societies, paternity is always "spiritual," just as is maternity, since it does not suppose the transmission only of genetic "capital," but also of an ensemble of possibilities that may be accepted or refused, but that nonetheless form the framework for the future development of those newly born. We know that in certain archaic societies, there was no established relation between the sexual act and procreation. This is proof that the linkage is by no means self-evident, and in any case, such a linkage is not sufficient to create true relations of filiation. Filiation is likewise of a spiritual essence, as witnessed in the richer countries by the ever-increasing practices of adoption and medically assisted pregnancy and birth, which require the intermediary of anonymous sperm donors and surrogate mothers. And cloning, which we cannot help but think that despite the prohibitions and cautions will one day be applied to humans, is not at all a mode of the perfect reproduction of a being who will have then been saved from death, as one sometimes imagines it. What differentiates the individual from his or her clone would specifically be their varying places in time and in the social world, which shape individuals as much as does biology.

The link that joins generations thus turns out to be more spiritual than biological, and true transmission is thus not a transmission of blood, but rather of knowledge and of the possibilities of life that it allows. This is why humans try to survive as much through their works as through their children. In this regard, transmitting knowledge, values, or a conception of life is just as important to them, if not more so. Their concern is to leave a trace in the memory of others, to survive not only in the flesh, but also and above all in spirit. Their immortality in the great beyond is not what matters; what does matter is their spectral living on in collective memory. Here, with this, we become aware of the fact that what essentially characterizes human life is coexistence with other humans, not only with our contemporaries who share the same span of time, but also and above all with those who have come before and those who will come after us. The shadows of the dead, like the shadows of those not yet born, accompany the human being in an invisible manner throughout its existence. And this virtual community is the true ground of all cultures. There is culture in the large sense of the term only when a struggle is engaged against the irreversibility of time, which implies the putting to work of a whole multitude of technologies destined to make up for forgetfulness; the first and most fundamental of these technologies is nothing other than language, which allows for the organization and transmission of experience.

Human time cannot be compared to a river, to the natural flowing of a flux leading us without obstacle from the past to the present; on the contrary, human time is made up of a multitude of discontinuous durations that must be brought into accord. The continuity of a shared history within a family or a nation can be gained only through a dialogue that puts the discontinuity of individual experiences in relation, a discontinuity whose extreme form is death. The dead person is in essence the one who no longer "responds" in the living dialogue, which endlessly requires being recommenced by each of the participants and which is now definitively interrupted. Merely inheriting the goods that the dead leave us is not sufficient to constitute a transmission from them to us; we must also feel ourselves called upon by the dead and accept responsibility for what is bequeathed to us. Following Heidegger, Gadamer clearly underlined in his analysis of the phenomenon of tradition[8] that transmission does not consist of a simple transfer of material goods from one subject to another and from one epoch to the next, because what is truly transmitted is less the content of an experience than the experience itself, insofar as it constitutes a possible form of being in the world. This kind of transmission, which supposes the reciprocal implication of the partners in play, is more of an *example* than it is a model to follow. What is truly transmitted is not so much an objective and reproducible knowledge as a *savoir-faire*, a know-how, to be appropriated and adapted.

We must not be too hasty to see in the works of the dead—monuments, writings, archives of any sort—the sole vectors of transmission. These contain mere residues of a past experiences that, if we are to understand their meaning, must in some way be led back to life by making them enter into a new experience. We understand on this basis the privilege given to oral tradition by certain societies—including our own, which has not yet replaced educators with robots.[9] Plato, the most illustrious representative of such an attitude in the Western world, saw in writing the mere simulacrum of true knowledge.[10] Yet writing—that is, the consignment of living speech permitting the conservation of what is transmitted beyond the death of the speaker—is born from the concern to make up for the transitory character of oral transmission. It makes possible the miracle of a "virtual communication."[11] We must recognize that writing is not a mere addition that would change nothing in the course of the oral tradition; it is rather the highest form of the neutralization of death, because it permits a quasi-immediate transmission. This is not the case with other vestiges of the past, for which the personal experience to which they belong must be reconstituted in order to understand their meaning. What is proper to writing, in contrast to monuments, is that it is comprehensible in itself and that there is no need to give a meaning to it. Literature, in the large sense of the word, including all forms of written communication, thus allows temporal distance to be abolished and institutes a virtual contemporaneity between the writer and the reader. But this is not a matter of a simple interpersonal relation similar to the kind we can have in dialogue, but rather of a common participation in the meaning of a text existing by itself and that is thus free with respect to both its author and its recipient. The horizon of meaning unfolded by the written is thus not limited by the actual author or reader. What is fixed by writing is therefore detached from the contingency of its origin and opened to new relations into which it can enter. Understood in this way, literature constitutes something like a sphere of universal and infinite meaning open to all those who know how to read.[12]

Could there be some possible access to immortality in this? To consider this question, we would have to replace "the beyond" with history and replace divine being with society. This is what happened in the nineteenth century with Marx, who proclaims that for humans, human being is the supreme being,[13] and also with Auguste Comte, who founds a "religion of humanity."[14] Favored by the growth of the bourgeoisie, the glorious myth of immortality blossomed in France, where toward the end of the eighteenth century, in the footprint of the old Sainte-Geneviève church, we constructed a building, the Pantheon, dedicated, as its name in no way suggests, to the memory of great men, and where today we call the members of the Académie française, that other temple devoted to the goddess Literature since the seventeenth century, the forty "Immortals."

We would, however, be wrong to sacralize writing and to believe in the redemptive power of written works. But even if to a certain extent these works constitute the "glorious body" of their dead creator and engender a devotion quite similar to the kind that we had previously reserved for deities, they are nevertheless as perishable as the material on which they are written. There are many examples in history of how we can indeed sacrifice ourselves to the work and grant it an absolute value. But this would also specifically mean recognizing that the work can live on without its creator, who in some way then disappears into his or her own creation. As the poet René Char said so well, "the design of poetry is to make us sovereign while depersonalizing us,"[15] so much so that as soon as the work has entered into collective memory, the poet becomes forgotten. There is in every work, and singularly in the literary work, a moment when its author becomes foreign to himself and considers himself, so to speak, already dead. We understand on this basis in what sense Derrida was able to say that writing is of a "testamentary essence."[16] But then writing is addressed only to those who survive us, and who themselves will also die.

Transmission, whether it be through genes, experience, or written works, therefore allows us at best only a temporary foreswearing of death, without which no culture and no history would be possible. What's at stake is a stratagem that is at the very origin of human becoming. There are, however, some less glorious ruses by means of which individuals try daily to circumvent death.

Illusory Immortality: The Cult of the Body, Risky Behavior, and Celebrity

Death comes to us via the body. We witness the body changing and aging over time, and through its decrepitude, we feel its forces and its influence over things waning. The desire to preserve and extend youth as long as possible is no doubt as old as humanity. But humanity can now take comfort in the belief that the progress of science can help in this respect. We now look to the pharmacopeia for the means to realize the dream of eternal youth. All this attention to the body in contemporary societies no doubt arises from the decline of belief in the existence and powers of the soul. But this does not in any way mean that the dualist vision of human being that had so profoundly marked the Christian West has been overcome. Quite to the contrary, it has been reinforced.

This will to master and even to transform the body that is so openly expressed today makes manifest our contemporaries' inability to consider the phenomenon of incarnation as self-evident. It is true that in sickness and aging, we suddenly become aware of the separation established between self and body. But there is quite a distance between these intermittent experiences of the duality of the body and mind and the will, which is now manifest everywhere, to look at one's body only through the eyes of the other and to model it according to the other's desire. Even though contemporary philosophy since Nietzsche has wanted to persuade human being that it *is* its body,[17] it seems in contrast that the only possible relation to the body has for some decades now become a relation of *having*, of *possessing* a malleable object. As David Le Breton very rightly notes, the body becomes the "prosthesis of an ego eternally in quest of a provisory incarnation in order to assure a meaningful trace of the self."[18]

Humans use their bodies differently, depending on their societies, which also attests to the fact that the body is not in any way reducible to its merely biological functions. Even more strikingly, emotional gestures and mimicry do not at all constitute natural signs, but instead differ depending on the populations in which they are made.[19] The totality of the human body, as of the expressivity of the marks that it makes on itself (such as tattooing, painting, and ritual mutilation), participates in the order of culture, and so it is not at all a question of wanting to return to a "nature" that human being had already definitively left behind the moment it made its appearance. Nonetheless, the objectification of the body has been carried to its highest point in our hypertechnological societies.

It is indeed in order to give body to one's existence and to conjure away what is most profoundly transitory about it that we multiply the corporeal signs addressed to the only kind of transcendence that we still recognize, the transcendence of the social milieu to which we belong. This goes for one's "look" or sense of style, as well as for the remodeling of the body by plastic surgery or by bodybuilding. All of these aim at a mastery over the body, a mastery that would like to deprive it of anything arising from the passivity in it that makes incarnation into a destiny to be assumed, rather than a choice that could someday be revoked. We ought not be surprised to see the idea of a "supernumerary" body appear here in the milieu of cyberculture,[20] nor is it even a matter of transforming the body through disguise; instead, the body is simply eliminated in order to allow a total immersion in a virtual reality freed entirely from any obstruction attached to corporeity. The entire discourse about the end of the body[21] (a notion that is also linked to the strange mystique of artificial intelligence) is the outcome of the dualist conception of human being imposed in the West since the beginning of modern times. It is indeed because the concept of the body as machine has been dominant since the seventeenth century that a regenerative medicine today gives itself the task of indefinitely extending the body's functioning. And because such science ultimately proves impotent to insure the promised amortality of the body, we are not surprised to see, even in the minds of eminent physicists, the appearance of the idea of a dematerialization of intelligence and even its transplantation into supports other than living matter.[22]

Modernity's cult of the body thus turns against itself and becomes its opposite, engendering distrust of this poorly performing instrument. We find the same distrust for this being of flesh and blood that we are in all risky behavior, which is another form of flirting with death. We are here, too, facing a sort of paradox: since the seventeenth century and the invention of life insurance—which, as Heidegger correctly emphasizes, is due to Leibniz, that is, to the thinker who first formulated the principle of sufficient reason and thus gave a foundation to modern science and technology in their search for a calculability integral to all things[23]—the concern for safety has never stopped increasing in Western societies and has become a veritable obsession in our era. Yet it is exactly in this context that risky activities are valorized, as is shown by the interest aroused by extreme sports in our societies. Those who choose to participate in them are in search of powerful feelings that have been totally stifled by the organization and planification of modern life in both the professional and the private domains. Their concern in freely putting their lives at stake is to give themselves the feeling of a plenitude of being that their overprotected existence no longer allows them to experience. But this kind of defiance of death is, paradoxically, a stratagem that is hatched in order to escape death, because it is accompanied by a feeling of omnipotence, which is the opposite of a true assumption of finitude. We cannot order or command death, but we can and do provoke it with the intention of escaping the absolute power it has over us, who, come what may, are nonetheless fated to die someday. This is why suicide, whatever its justification, may not really consist in killing oneself, but should perhaps rather be viewed as an attempt to dodge death. Whoever chooses suicide refuses with the same gesture to be mortal, refuses to allow death to come upon him or her without reason or to attack him or her like a fatality. To kill oneself is perhaps to want to affirm one's own immortality and to propose implicitly that death can depend on one's own will: here again, there is an astonishing paradox. Suicide no doubt finds justification in certain limit cases, but it always remains a final parry against death, since it consists in allowing oneself to believe that one has freely chosen what nevertheless always remains an inexorable destiny in the face of whose reality the human being is totally impotent.

These deliberate games with death or risky behaviors such as rock climbing, parachuting, and solitary navigation or exploration may offer the possibility of restoring meaning and intensity to life, but they do not fundamentally differ from the risky behaviors that include drug abuse, alcoholism, excessive speed on the road, bad diet, and all other forms of refusal of social integration.[24] The same lack of being is experienced in the two cases, for which one seeks to compensate by heroically proving one's existence to oneself or that one tries to escape by neutralizing the feeling of physical limits. This kind of self-testing and deliberate search for danger has certainly always constituted a rite of passage to adulthood in traditional societies, and it is obvious that they contribute essentially to the construction of personal identity. Hegel gave philosophical form to what appears to be an anthropological constant in his famous dialectic of master and slave by showing that in the struggle in which each puts his life at stake, whoever goes furthest in their disregard for death attains self-consciousness.[25] But there is a margin between the rites of initiation, as dangerous as they are, and this risk taking that is approvingly marked with the seal of modern individualism. The former are a factor in social integration, while the latter are symptoms of the disintegration of a society whose members no longer maintain private relations with death.

This does not, however, mean that the intersubjective dimension is totally absent from these games with death. Exposing oneself voluntarily to death by giving oneself over to extreme sports is a manner of showing one's superiority to others. And a number of risky behaviors are calls for help, unspoken demands for aid, or appeals to one's friends. One slips away from the radical forsakenness accompanying a true confrontation with death by continuing to situate oneself in relation to the judgment of others. This is why another way to give oneself the illusion of immortality is to become the point of convergence of every gaze—by becoming a celebrity. The concern here is not a search for glory, or a desire to inscribe one's name in history, or the creation of works likely to be passed on to posterity, but rather an attempt to find immediate relief from one's sickness of being by asking others [*autrui*] for a testimony to one's existence.

Our epoch is characterized by an "obsession with the other"[26] because it is profoundly marked by the development of individualism. There is only an apparent paradox in this: the relation to the other becomes obsessive only when it is no longer self-evident, only when a being-in-common or existence shared with others appears no longer as a factual given, but rather as a problem to resolve or a task to accomplish. We must add to that the increasing disappearance from our societies of the dimension of transcendence. Unable to grant itself divine being by transcendence, which so cruelly makes the finite creature into the defective being that it is, humans turn toward others.[27] We must certainly recognize, as Hannah Arendt did, that appearing is an essential dimension of existence and that "nothing and nobody exists in the world whose very being does not presuppose a *spectator*."[28] But it is not sufficient to be looked at in order to be; on the contrary, it is because existence makes itself visible that it necessarily offers itself to the gaze. The case is completely different in what we call "the society of the spectacle,"[29] in which there is no other possibility for being except in the gaze of others, which is an extreme form of alienation, that is, of becoming foreign to oneself. Yet this is what is obscurely sought in celebrity: self-objectification, identification of the self with one's public image in order to be alleviated of the burden of one's finitude. As Sartre—who was the first to grant a capital importance to the gaze, going so far as to claim that "the other is in principle *the one who looks at me*"[30]—rightly emphasizes, the sensation of being looked at does not necessarily suppose the effective presence of the one who looks, which implies that it is impossible to situate the source of the gaze in the world.[31] We understand on this basis how we can lend to the Other (now written with a capital) a ubiquity and omnipotence quite similar to those of a transcendent God. But here it is simply a question of what Heidegger rightly called the "dictatorship of the public realm,"[32] to which whoever desires celebrity is entirely subjected, to the point of having the feeling of a total annihilation of their being when the public's favor is lost.

The impasse to which this extreme form of alienation (comparable to what leads to the frantic search for power in the games of finance, of the political, or of seduction) testifies to the illusory character of all of the attempts at the neutralization of death. Though human being has admirably tried very hard to lie to itself, there is always that moment when the veils of illusion are torn asunder, and human being is summoned to accept its mortal condition.

3

Accepting Death

What does "accepting" death mean here? The French term for this, *assumer*, refers to how one takes on or appropriates one's own death for oneself—for this is indeed the primary meaning of the Latin verb *adsumere*. Is it a question, when facing an ineluctable destiny, of resigning oneself to it, or, on the contrary, of recognizing in it the very ground of one's being? Is it a question of anticipating in thought the future event of one's demise, or, on the contrary, of existing (in the transitive sense of the verb) in one's mortal condition. We see that this taking charge of death can have different meanings, depending on whether one considers death as the last episode of human life, or, in contrast, as an essential attribute of human life.

Preparation for Death: Christianity and Philosophy

Rather than living under the illusion of one's own immortality and trying to overcome or neutralize death, we can instead choose to look it directly in the face and prepare to confront it when it comes. We ought not be surprised if this attitude has been recommended in the West by the Christian religion. What is specific to Christianity is the importance it gives to death, despite the promises of immortality and eternal life that it also offers. What is at the heart of its foundational ritual is the death of Christ, that is, the death of a god who, by being incarnated in the person of Jesus, has accepted to take on the finite condition of the human. What Jesus experiences in the garden of Gethsemane is the forsakenness and anxiety that are the lot of anyone dying.[1] And the sufferings of his human agony are exemplified in the innumerable crucifixes and in the pietàs found everywhere in the Christian world. This spectacle of the Passion of the Christ, which Christians constantly have before their eyes, endlessly enjoins them to remember that death is what constitutes the very essence of their being. To live as a Christian is to live in the imminence of death, which, as Saint Paul says in an oft-cited passage from the First Letter to the Thessalonians, "will come like a thief in the night" without one's knowing in advance either the day or the hour.[2]

Every Christian is therefore invited to meditate on death, and this meditation will even constitute what is essential to piety and devotion as the monastic orders develop, along with their doctrine of a "contempt for the world."[3] Bearing witness to this is the major work of Christian spirituality dating from the fifteenth century, the *Imitation of Jesus Christ*, which was for many centuries and until 1960 the most read Christian book in the world after the Bible.[4] There is thus in the Christian perspective an entire art of dying well, which must be developed in the dying individual by exhorting him or her to pray for the salvation of his or her soul and to resist the temptation of despair. The emphasis is placed on the very moment of death, which is when one most runs the risk of seeing the doors to eternal life being closed. The best way to combat the terror accompanying the last moment of life, however, is to habituate oneself ahead of time to the idea that one will someday have to enter this last stage. Beginning in the seventeenth century, all the literature dedicated to the preparation for death that develops in Catholic Europe is centered on the idea that one must get accustomed to death and dispel through meditation the fear that it produces. It is interesting in this regard to see Fénélon in his *Traité de l'éducation des filles* [Treatise on the education of girls] counseling the nuns to speak of death to children, to show them not only tombs, but also the dead themselves, as well as the grieving;[5] today, in contrast, perhaps out of fear that the emotions are too powerful, we hide the spectacle of death from children and try to keep them away from funeral ceremonies. The evocation of the corpse, including the most horrible details, was meant to persuade true believers that they are in exile on this earth and that their bodies are but prisons.

For Christianity, death is a passage, and the throes of the Passion are succeeded by the joy of the Resurrection. The Christian God, who by dying triumphs over death, is a god who "restores the dead to life" and who enjoins mortals to hope "against all hope."[6] The entire tragedy of the human condition, which is symbolized by the death on the cross of the Son of God abandoned by his Father, is thus suddenly both justified and abolished at the same time. As Saint Paul once again forcefully says, "the dead will be raised imperishable," "the mortal has clothed itself in immortality," because "death has been swallowed up in victory," and it will then be time to proclaim "Oh death, where is thy victory? Oh death, where is thy sting?"[7] The metaphor is clear: for the believer, death has lost its sting, and this whole fascination with the macabre, which is a constant feature of Christianity, has free reign only because death has been forever vanquished. The acceptance of death here has the dialectical form of a recognition that is at the same time a denial.

Yet is there not another, more serene way to prepare oneself for death, and isn't it what philosophy taught us well before Christianity? It is not without importance that the birth of philosophy is tied to the dramatic event of the death of its founder, Socrates, which Plato recounts to us in the *Phaedo*, a dialogue specifically dedicated to the question of the immortality of the soul in which a conception of death entirely different from the one proposed by Greek mythology is inaugurated. Plato declares that there is a certain identity between death and philosophy in the sense that both have the effect of untying the soul from the body. Thought is a symbolic death, because the human being must in some way die in body, or at least leave it behind, in order to access the immortality of the spirit. What is required of the philosopher is that he or she take care concerning death and make an effort to die,[8] which does not imply preparing for the ineluctable event that death is, but rather applying oneself throughout life to separate one's soul from the body, as Plato subsequently clearly specifies.[9] The question is thus not that of "learning how to die," as Montaigne will later say, but rather of being concerned "with dying and being dead"[10] in this life in order to be born into the only life worth living, the life of thought. What distinguishes the philosopher is that he or she does not fear death. The fear of death comes not from true knowledge, but rather from a common opinion held by those immersed in sensuous life, which is the belief in a total destruction of their being after death. Whoever has the experience of thinking through bodily death on the contrary discovers in this very exercise the indestructibility of the soul. The philosophical strategy whose matrix we find here consists, as we have seen, in transforming the fear of death into a fear of life, because what all philosophers fear above all is not leaving this life, but rather of living with too great an attachment to the body and to the sensuous. The true danger therefore resides for the philosopher in granting bodily death too great an importance. But if philosophizing consists in being one of the living dead, then philosophical life consequently has the explicit meaning of a victory won over death, which is thus dispossessed of its radical negativity.

Must we believe that the philosopher, who loves knowledge, but doesn't possess it,[11] is really able to escape from the world of common opinion? In truth, the philosopher is alone in considering sensuous life and the body itself as a prison. And thought does not *really* liberate the philosopher from this captivity, but does have the effect of making him or her aware of it. It is only by becoming aware of her or her own finitude that the thinker is able to open himself or herself to the infinity of the mind. Human thought is thus *both* the overcoming *and* the acceptance of finitude *at the same time*. This explains why we do not find any truly convincing proofs of the immortality of the soul in the *Phaedo*. Plato cannot truly claim that the soul is immortal, because that would go beyond what a mortal can know. He simply declares that there is an *interest* to bet on immortality and to live *as if* the soul were immortal, because if immortality really exists, we will have been right, and if it doesn't, we will at least have led a worthy life by refusing to remain a slave to our senses. He thus initiates what will become the fundamental trait of Western thought, to the point that later, in that other summit of philosophical thought that is

German Idealism, we will be able to identify philosophy with idealism. But we can also see in Platonism the origin of the devaluation of the sensuous and of bodily life that will later lead Christianity to advocate a contempt for the world and the flesh. Pascal is not wrong when he notes in one of his *Pensées* that we need Plato to "be disposed toward Christianity."[12]

Already in Plato, the exercise of dying in one's bodily life ends up robbing death of its sting, making it inoffensive or even allowing it us to "get used to" it, as Montaigne will later say, thereby inscribing himself in this great tradition going back to Plato and the Stoics. Montaigne is, truthfully speaking, closest to the Stoics above all, since for him, the concern is not at all to devalue sensuous life to the benefit of the life of the mind, but on the contrary, to be reconciled with nature and with fate. This is the meaning that we must give to the formula that serves as a title for one of the chapters of the *Essays*, "That to Philosophize Is to Learn to Die."[13] For Montaigne, learning how to die consists in enabling oneself to confront the crucial moment of death by seeing in it the "master day," "the day that is the judge of all the others."[14] This is why it is a matter of our working to vanquish the fear of death, which is "due only to fantasy,"[15] also known as the imagination. The fear of death is therefore absurd—and here Montaigne turns to Epicurus, and takes up his major argument—because death "does not concern you dead or alive: alive because you are, dead because you are no more."[16] The concern is to take away death's strangeness, to get used to the idea of the inevitable; to do this, it is a matter of representing it "at every moment . . . in our imagination in all its aspects."[17] The more we think about death, the more it imposes itself on our thinking and the less it will have influence over us. Montaigne thus avows, concerning a serious accident that brought him close to death, that "in order to get used to the idea of death . . . there is nothing like coming close to it."[18]

Montaigne therefore seems to rejoin the Christian concern to prepare for the decisive moment of death. His long meditation on death had led him to understand that death accompanies us throughout life and that it is therefore not simply the end of life. He recognizes that "the continual work of our life is to build death," and he claims that we are in death while we are in life, so that consequently, "death affects the dying much more roughly than the dead, and more keenly and essentially."[19] He inaugurates an entirely different conception of mortality, no longer based on the critical moment of death, but rather on dying understood as the fundamental mode of being human, a conception that is the foundation for the entire analysis of being-toward-death that Heidegger develops in *Being and Time*.

For we must not identify death and dying. Death, as we have seen, is a phenomenon that is part of life and as such is accessible only to the kind of thinking that "looks on from above" [*pensée du survol*] that is characteristic of scientific thought.[20] The human being can certainly be viewed, for example, as one living being among others, as an object of biological science, or, insofar as the human being is the animal that buries its dead, as an object of the human sciences. A whole variety of research concerning death can be developed from this perspective. But this is possible only because the researcher already knows from his or her own experience what death is. If the researcher did not already have this awareness of death, no objective event arising in the world could ever be able to put him or her in relation to it. For what essentially characterizes human being is the relation to its own death, which can never become an event in the world, since it constitutes the end of the world for the human being. The end can appear to the human being in the figure of a mundane or worldly event—which we might call a passing-away or a demise—only from the moment that he or she views it from the outside, as if it were a question of the death of another. It is in no way a matter here of denying the possibility and validity of a biology, a psychology, a sociology, and an anthropology of death, but rather simply of showing the unperceived presupposition on which they rest, the understanding that human being has of itself as a mortal. For human being can have access to death "in general" only through awareness of its own mortality.

Wanting to prepare oneself for death is thus possible only to the extent that one has already made death into an event and identified dying with mere demise. One has therefore already been given an insurance policy against death, since one can then be considered immortal as long as death is not there. We live, moreover, in this provisory immortality most of the time, and it is legitimate to think that human existence can unfurl all its potentialities only insofar as it tries to overcome or to neutralize death and is capable of transforming the very foundation of its existence into an event yet to come. What we lie about to and hide from ourselves on a daily basis is the *imminence* of death, the fact that it is possible *at any moment* and that the indetermination of the moment of death is not separable from the certainty of death. In the end, only this inauthentic postponement of death allows death to be confused with demise, with this mundane event that happens only to others. But then what would it mean to exist in the imminence of one's own death? What would it mean to exist as mortal?

Existing as Mortal

Is it really possible to accept death, that is, to take charge of one's own mortality, without lying to oneself about it? Are

we not, on the contrary, constantly dedicated to dissimulat-
ing it to ourselves, living the illusion of our own immortality? Since its birth, philosophy has defined itself as an
attempt to be authentically open to the extreme possibility
that death is open to it by coming close to it in thought.
But by the very fact that this meditation on death, as Montaigne says, involves "coming close to " death or getting
"used to" it, death is still commanded by a will to assure a
certain mastery over it, thereby stripping it of the horror it
engenders. The same goes for our anxiously awaiting death,
which transforms death into a possibility to be worried
about or concerned with, implying its relativization: to be
concerned with death, in religious or philosophical meditations, thus consists in transforming it into one possibility
among others.

But if death thereby appears as the unthinkable itself,
would one then have to say that we should instead turn
away from the false ideas that we can have of it, such as the
false fears that it can engender, and deliberately refuse to
take account of the possibility of it? This is the position of
certain philosophers, and in particular, of Spinoza, who declares that "the free man thinks of nothing less than death,
and his wisdom is a meditation on life, not on death."[21] But
this claim coexists in Spinoza with the commonly and
widely held conviction that death can therefore be avoided
because it has a grip on only one single part of our being,
the perishable part. This is the same Spinoza who claims
that "the human mind cannot be absolutely destroyed with
the body, but something of it remains which is eternal"[22]—
something that is certainly not the soul as a personal entity,
but is rather the mind or universal reason. This is because
we participate by our understanding in universal reason: despite the finitude of our corporal and sensuous existence,
"we feel and know by experience that we are eternal."[23] As

we can see, the best way to anaesthetize the fright that the thought of our mortality evokes in us is to appeal to what is impersonal and nonsensuous in us, to what the Greeks called *logos* and the Romans named *reason*. Situated in this same perspective is Boëtius, that thinker from the end of antiquity, the great translator of Greek into Latin, to whom the Scholastic philosophers owe a huge part of their terminology, and the author of a book that remained famous throughout the Middle Ages, *The Consolations of Philosophy*, a work he wrote in prison while awaiting death.

But do we really need to be consoled or to tear ourselves away from our sensuous attachments in order to be able to vanquish the anxiety that death induces in us? We are once again dealing here with the same strategy already defended by Plato, which for the human being consists in separating out the passions and cultivating only pure thought. This is also the same Plato, however, who gave a great deal of place to sensuousness in philosophizing itself, which he conceives as a love of knowledge, itself grounded in a specific emotion, wonder, and which sometimes even leads the thinker into madness, as when he finally achieves the vision of the Idea.[24] What else would the experience of thought be if it were not an *elevation* above and beyond the contingencies of daily life, an *exaltation* of our whole being? But understanding that such a transport could happen only thanks to, and not despite, our bodily and earthly anchorage demands a "revolution in the way of thinking" that the first rationalist to consider sensibility as a source of knowledge and the first thinker of radical finitude, Immanuel Kant, tried to promote.

We believe that confronting death requires a sort of heroism. But it is about this heroism that the major misinterpretation of the Heideggerian thought of being-toward-death is habitually made. Such heroism is in no way a matter of getting "used to the idea of death," or of hardening oneself against it, or of considering it as an inevitable evil that one must stoically prepare oneself to endure. Despite every appeal to cold reason, our relation to death remains marked by horror. Death is not dominated by thought. The idea that we may free ourselves from the anxiety that arises from our being mortal merely by appealing to reason constitutes an illusion or trap that in the end is just as deceptive as any of the discourses about "the beyond" or technico-scientific fantasies about the indefinite extension of life. It is not a matter of quieting anxiety, or of "dedramatizing" death, or of attaining a state of *ataraxia* with respect to death, that is, the total absence of disquiet or disturbance that both Stoicism and Epicureanism recommended to those seeking happiness. Nor is it a question of amputating the sensitive part of our being that is upset by the thought of death. We must instead stop opposing anxiety with vain resistances and let ourselves be borne by it in order thus to achieve that moment when it changes into joy. Such a transmutation occurs both in us and without us; it happens without us causing it. The best word to describe such a change of state would be the word of the great German mystic of the thirteenth and fourteenth centuries, Meister Eckhart, who spoke of *Gelassenheit*, a letting be that lets all things return to themselves at the moment one stops making use of them for one's projects, the moment when one is able to deprive oneself of one's ego. What Meister Eckhart calls "detachment" or "letting be" or "releasement" cannot be identified with the Stoic notion of *ataraxia*: it is the state characteristic of one who has separated himself or herself from common opinions and common fears, not through the violent refusal of his or her own finitude, but rather in order to be opened to its truth. This calm before death, which religions and philosophies have assigned as the supreme goal of human life, is less the work of asceticism than of detachment, and we may be able to achieve it not by situating ourselves beyond anxiety, but rather by accepting the possibility that we can remain within anxiety, as in the still zone at the center of whirlwinds.

What does it mean for us that our lifetime is limited, that there is a beginning and an end? In the monotheistic tradition, which conceives the one and only God as omnipotent and infinite, the limited and finite have constantly been conceived as a form of imperfection. An abyss is therefore dug between God and his creatures. It is on this basis that death appears as a kind of inherent defect in the human condition. We can then perhaps understand why Meister Eckhart, for whom God may be unattainable by reason, but may yet be united with man through a mystical union, was condemned by the Inquisition. In the monotheistic horizon that from the beginning of the Christian era has dominated the Western tradition, human finitude is thinkable only in contrast with divine infinity. The self-understanding that finite being has would come to it from its relation with the infinite Other. This is exactly what takes place in classical philosophy, still subservient to theology, and in particular in the work of René Descartes. Descartes, discovering the idea of infinity in himself, conceives of the finitude of human being on the basis of divine existence, and not on the basis of the mortality of the subject.[25] Kant himself, the first modern philosopher explicitly to refuse to take the hypothesis of a creator God as his point of departure, nevertheless continues to understand human finitude in an exterior fashion, in opposition to what could be a divine infinity. In order to think finitude in its truth, Kant should no longer have begun from the idea of this infinite and wholly positive being that the transcendent God of Revelation is. Have we not sufficiently remarked in this respect that "in-finite" is a negative word that supposes the overcoming of limits—

that it is *first of all* a matter of opening a way? Does not starting thus from the infinite and giving it primacy consist in taking things the wrong way? This is what becomes clear when we turn to the ancient Greeks who, outside of the monotheistic tradition, developed a wholly different conception of the finite, identified with the perfect, and of the limit, understood not in an exterior fashion (as that on the basis of which something ceases or stops), but rather as that in which a thing has its origin and finds its stability.

The question of understanding the being of humans would therefore begin from its end, its death. We would then have access to the idea of a radical finitude that no longer rests on the presupposition of a beyond of time nor arises from the ground of a preceding infinite. Dying could then appear as the very condition of our being born and mortality as *a chance* for the human being—no longer an obstacle, but rather the springboard from which the human can then leap into existence. We would then understand that human beings remain, most often without knowing it, in intimate relation with this possibility, which is their own, of no longer being in the world, of the total closure to being—this abyssal obscurity from which it emerged and to which it will return. What would then have occurred is the human's becoming aware that the essential transitoriness and precariousness of its being is also what allows it to be open to itself, to others, and to the world. Death would then no longer appear as a scandal, but rather as the very foundation of our existence.

Is such a conversion of attitude possible in the world today, where the struggle for the self-affirmation of the human is accomplished in the form of a will to planification, to calculation, and to the supervision of all things? For this change to occur, the technicized animal that the human is becoming would have to return to the human realm and accept *leaving room for* the incalculable, the irremediable, and all the negativity that existence can contain. This would in no way mean some kind of reconciliation with death, which no matter what we do, preserves its foreignness and strangeness. But it could mean that we gain access to a more relaxed relation with the ineluctable, with the human being's acceptance of its own finitude, *which always also means its incomparable singularity.* For it is this relation with its own always imminent death that makes the human being something other than a mere living being, that is, a mere particularization of universal life. This relation to death grants it a history and makes of its existence something other than the predictable unfolding of a program, and it is this singular history that finds its "end" in death.

Restoring to death its irremedial, nonrelational, and nonsubstitutable character makes the relation to death become once again a relation that a *singular* being has to its *own* death—and this relation should also be what promulgates a true medical *art*, a veritable *therapeia* or "care" and "service" rendered by the medical doctor to his fellow human beings, to whom he is devoted.[26] For the therapeutic relation in the fullest sense can be truly understood only as a relation to *a mortal*, and not to a merely living being. At least in the so-called developed countries, death has become for most people an anonymous death in the hospital or clinic—one of the principal tasks of hospital facilities today being the production of cadavers[27]—and it is to the omnipotence of technology that we owe the practice of the artificial extension of life and the reduction of human being to a mere organism, maintaining its vegetative functions with the help of machines or by the prescription of powerful anesthetics. We must dare to say that, paradoxically, the concern to extend the life of a human being at any price can be the expression of a real denial of her humanity. Such a concern views death as not belonging to human being, seeing it as an "accident" that an all-powerful medical science may able to avoid or even indefinitely defer. In such a perspective, death, given back to its impersonal exterior, could only ever be passively submitted to by the patient and could only be considered a personal failure by the caregiver. The total passivity of the sick person with respect to the onset of a radically exterior event on which the person has no grip and with which there is no relation corresponds to the doctor's presumption in imagining himself to be the efficient cause of the survival of the sick, even though he or she is only ever assisting the occasion of such survival.[28]

Given that medicine has not yet been able to find a palliative for such a death merely undergone, could we substitute the idea of an accepted death? Or of a "good" death? This is the whole reason that, starting in the 1960s, so-called "palliative" care was put in place.[29] What such a substitution would imply for hospital technologies is an entirely different understanding of the therapeutic relation, which would now be viewed as that of *one mortal to another mortal*. The solicitude owed to a mortal cannot consist for the doctor in *substituting* himself or herself for the sick, that is, in discharging the sick of concern for his or her death and thereby aiming to make him or her dependent. On the contrary, it consists in *helping the patient take charge of his or her own mortal existence*. Only such solicitude[30] is truly capable of giving the patient back a dignity that relegation to the level of a "clinical case"—from the moment of his or her entry into the hospital structure—has ineluctably made the patient lose. We must forcefully underline that the relation to the *patient as a singular being* does not depend so much on the quality of "objective" care that surrounds her as on the way in which we allow her *to accept by herself* her own existence as a mortal. This is possible only if the physician or therapist refuses to be confined to the impersonal role of the one who holds objective knowledge and instead accepts sharing with his patient the same *vulnerability* that makes both of them mortals. The consequence of such a conception of the medical art and of therapy would be that in the application of his acquired competence, the doctor does not behave *only* as a technician or scientist, but *also* as a human, a mortal. Only this reform of the medical art could guarantee to the dying today a truly humane "end of life," especially in developed countries.

ↄ

"Become who you are." Nietzsche's injunction, borrowed from Pindar,[31] is addressed to humankind, to whom he wanted to teach, through his *Zarathustra*, the meaning of the earth.[32] Heidegger situates himself in the same perspective when he calls humanity to this transmutation of its being, which will make a mortal out of the rational animal.[33] *Becoming* a mortal would require that we stop giving in to the illusions of immortality and become capable of truly living on the earth and dwelling in a body. Becoming mortal would then no longer be merely confronting death and looking it in the face, but rather *being able* to die, and thereby seeing in death not an imperfection of the human being, but on the contrary, a capacity.[34] On this basis, it could also be revealed to human beings that anxiety in the face of death is in no way incompatible with the joy of existing.

Notes

Foreword

1. Friedrich Nietzsche, *Also sprach Zarathustra*, in *Sämtliche Werke, Kritische Studienausgabe in 15 Bänden*, ed. Giorgio Colli and Mazzino Montinari (Berlin: Deutscher Taschenbuch Verlag and W. de Gruyter, 1980), 4:22. I have given myself the pleasure of translating these lines myself, but advise readers to get the wonderful translation of Nietzsche's *Thus Spoke Zarathustra* by Graham Parkes (Oxford: Oxford University Press, 2005) .

2. Albert Camus, *Le mythe de Sisyphe* (Paris: Gallimard, 1942), 40–41, cited in the Introduction to Martin Heidegger, *Basic Writings*, 2nd ed. (San Francisco: HarperCollins, 1993), 23.

3. Martin Heidegger, *Sein und Zeit*, 12th ed. (Tübingen: Niemeyer, 1972), sections 50–53. We have two translations of Heidegger's book, the first by John Macquarrie and Edward Robinson, published in 1962 by Harper and Row in New York and Blackwell's in England, the second by Joan Stambaugh, revised by Dennis J. Schmidt, published in 2010 by the State University of New York Press.

Introduction

1. Sigmund Freud, "Thoughts for the Times on War and Death," in *The Standard Edition of the Complete Psychological Works of Sigmund Freud*, ed. and trans. James Strachey, vol. 14, *On the History of Psycho-analytic Movement, Papers on Metapsychology and Other Works* (London: Hogarth Press, 1953–1974), 289.

2. Epicurus, "Letter to Menoeceus," in *Letters, Principal Doctrines, and Vatican Sayings*, ed. and trans. Russell Greer (New York: Bobbs-Merrill, 1964), 125.

3. [As Dastur explains in Chapter 3, the French word *assumer* has its roots in the Latin *adsumere*, which has the sense of resigning oneself to "taking on" something—a burden, for example, or responsibility for one's faults and failings. The English cognate "assumption" is not false, but ambiguous—though it is worth noting that even in the domain of logic, an assumption is a premise, perhaps contestable, that one takes on, that one accepts for the sake of argument—Trans.]

1. Overcoming Death

1. Among the cultures that practice exposure of the dead, we know above all that of the Zoroastrians, who expose their dead to the vultures atop the famous "towers of silence." See Françoise Dastur, "Le corps livré aux vautours: Les rites funéraires dans le zoroastrianisme" [The body thrown to the vultures: Funerary rites in Zoroastrianism], in *La mort et l'immortalité: Encyclopédie des savoirs et des croyances* [Death and immortality: The encyclopedia of knowledge and belief], ed. Frédéric Lenoir and Jean-Philippe de Tonnac (Paris: Bayard, 2004), 257–68.

2. The word used in the original French text is *défunt*, which comes from the Latin *defungor*, meaning "to accomplish, to acquit oneself of a task or a debt." *Defunctus* means "he who has left from," or "he who has finished or is done with something," and therefore, by extension, "the dead." [*Defunct* in English has the same Latin root. Dastur uses *défunt* frequently, but not exclusively, to speak of the dead person, differentiating its meaning

from "deceased" and "departed." Given the colloquial meaning of *defunct* in English, however, we have chosen to translate it as "deceased" throughout, despite the author's etymological considerations.—Trans.]

3. We see by the use of terms such as "the deceased" and "the departed" to designate death that death is considered as a departure toward an elsewhere or as a passage to another mode of existence.

4. It is in Mazdeism (from the name of the god Ahura Mazda, the wise lord), a religion of ancient Persia whose influence on Judaism and Christianity is proven, that we find the first representations of an end of time in the form of a last judgment as well as notions of "heaven" or "paradise" (a word of Persian origin that originally meant "garden") and "hell."

5. Karl Marx, "Contribution to the Critique of Hegel's *Philosophy of Right*," in Marx, *Critique of Hegel's 'Philosophy of Right,'* trans. and ed. J. J. O'Malley (Cambridge: Cambridge University Press, 1970), 131.

6. Friedrich Nietzsche, "On the Afterworldly," in *Thus Spoke Zarathustra*, first part, in *The Portable Nietzsche*, trans. and ed. Walter Kaufmann (New York: Viking, 1954), 142–43.

7. See Hans-Georg Gadamer, "The Experience of Death," in Gadamer, *The Enigma of Health,* trans. Jason Gaiger and Nicholas Walker (Stanford: Stanford University Press: 1996), 63.

8. See on this subject Philippe Ariès, *Western Attitudes toward Death: From the Middle Ages to the Present*, trans. Patricia A. Ranum (Baltimore: Johns Hopkins University Press, 1974).

9. Louis-Vincent Thomas, *Anthropologie de la mort* [Anthropology of death] (Paris: Payot, 1975), 525.

10. Jean-Hugues Dechaux, "Neutraliser l'effroi: Vers un nouveau régime de deuil" [Neutralizing fright: Toward a new regime of mourning], in *La mort et l'immortalité*, 1152–71.

11. See Edgar Morin, "L'homme et la mort" [Mankind and death] in *La mort et l'immortalité*, 41. The author recalls in this article that his essay published in 1951 under the same title had been a complete commercial disaster, because death was then a forbidden subject.

12. See Robert William Higgins, "La mort ophéline: La question de 'deuil impossible'" [Orphan death: The question of 'impossible mourning'"] in *La mort et l'immortalité.*, 1641–54.

13. The expression "work of mourning" is Freudian in origin. See Freud, "Mourning and Melancholia," in *Collected Papers IV*, ed. and trans. under the direction of Joan Rivière (New York: Basic Books, 1959). But just as the word "travail" (French for "work") which comes from the Latin *tripalium*, designating an instrument of torture, has the original sense of "torment," the German word *Arbeit* etymologically refers to the same idea of pain and suffering, and this is probably how Freud understood it and how we should understand Freud.

14. Although in Hinduism, cremation is used to place one in relation with belief in the transmigration of the soul, it is entirely different in contemporary societies, where cremation obeys much more pragmatic motifs and motives. See Jean-Dider Urbain, "La cendre et la trace: La vogue de la crémation" [Ashes and the trace: The vogue of cremation] in *La mort et l'immortalité*, 1207–32.

15. See the works of a psychoanalytic inspiration by Nicolas Abraham and Maria Torok, as well as the analysis given of them by Jacques Derrida in his essay "Fors," which prefaces Nicholas Abraham and Maria Torok, *Wolf Man's Magic Word: A Cryptonomy*, trans Nicholas Rand (Minneapolis: Minnesota University Press, 1986).

16. Plato, *Phaedo* 82e.

17. Keith Ansell Pearson, "The Incorporation of Truth: Towards the Overhuman," in *A Companion to Nietzsche*, ed. Keith Ansell Pearson (Malden: Blackwell, 2006), 235. [The French translation of *The Will to Power*, a posthumously assembled text with a well-documented history of unfortunate editorial decisions, does not correspond to the English translation; hence, here and in note 18 below, we refer the reader to secondary sources.—Trans.]

18. Friedrich Nietzsche, *The Will to* Power, quoted in Michel Haar, *Nietzsche and Metaphysics*, trans. Michael Gendre (Albany: State University of New York Press, 1996), 120.

19. See Spinoza, *Ethics* part 4, prop. 67, in *A Spinoza Reader: The "Ethics" and Other Works*, ed. and trans. Edwin Curley (Princeton: Princeton University Press, 1994), 235. As to Nietzsche, here is what he declares on the topic of the thought of death: "It makes me happy that men do not want at all to think about death. I should like very much to do something that would make the thought of life even a hundred times more appealing to them." Friedrich Nietzsche, *The Gay Science*, trans. Walter Kaufmann (New York: Vintage, 1974), book 4, section 278, 225.

20. "Full of resource against all that comes to him / Is Man. Against Death alone / He is left with no defence." Sophocles, *Antigone*, lines 360–62, in *Antigone, Oedipus the King, Electra*, ed. Edith Hall, trans. H. D. F. Kitto (New York: Oxford University Press, 1998), 14.

21. Hans Jonas, *The Imperative of Responsibility: In Search of an Ethics for the Technological Age* (Chicago: University of Chicago Press, 1984), 18.

22. M. F. X. Bichat, *Physiological Researches on Life and Death* (1800), in *Significant Contributions to the History of Psychology, 1750–1920*, series E, vol. 2, ed. Daniel N. Robinson (Washington, D.C.: University Publications of America, 1978), 10.

23. August Weismann, *Essays upon Heredity and Kindred Biological Problems*, vol. 1, ed. Edward B. Poulton, Selmar Schönland, and Arthur E. Shipley (Oxford: Clarendon Press, 1892), 25; the citation occurs in the midst of an extremely interesting discussion of biological death, 20–27. Also cited by André Klarsfeld and Frédéric Revah in *The Biology of Death: Origins of Mortality*, trans. Lydia Brady (Ithaca: Cornell University Press, 2004), where one also finds a helpful intellectual biography and assessment of Weismann's work, 12–20.

24. Klarsfeld and Revah, *The Biology of Death*, 8. Again, the citation is found in the midst of a helpful discussion of Lamarck's life and work, 6–9. The citation is from Lamarck, *Recherches sur l'organisation des corps vivants* [Research on the organization of living bodies] (1802).

25. See Jean-Claude Ameisen, "Dans l'oubli de nos metamorphoses: Aperçus sur les mécanismes d'autodestruction cellulaires"

[In the forgetfulness of our metamorphoses: Glimpses of autodestructive cellular mechanisms], in *La mort et l'immortalité*, 147071. See also by the same author *La sculpture du vivant: Le suicide cellulaire ou la mort créatrice* [The sculpture of the living: Cellular suicide or creative death] (Paris: Seuil, 2003).

26. See for all that follows the article by Nicolas Prantzos, "Vers le zéro absolu: Hypothèses sur la fin de l'univers" [Toward absolute zero: Hypotheses about the end of the universe], in *La mort et l'immortalité*, 1571–89.

2. Neutralizing Death

1. "Anxiety" comes from the Latin *augustia*, which means "narrow space" and refers to the part of the body that is particularly narrowed, the throat, an organ of swallowing but also of speech, which is properly human.

2. As Heidegger rightly underlined in *Being and Time,* section 53, death is "the possibility of the impossibility of existence" and anxiety is nothing other than the vertigo that seizes us before the abyss suddenly opening beneath our feet. Martin Heidegger, *Being and Time*, trans. Joan Stambaugh (Albany: State University of New York Press, 1996), 242.

3. See ibid., sections 51 and 52.

4. [The phrase "faire une parade" used in the original French here gains one of its meanings from the world of fencing, naming the active defensive strategy called a "parry," used to meet and deflect an attack. It can also mean "to parade" in the sense of both a political *manifestation*, a demonstration against something, and an entertaining distraction from something; one is also tempted to hear in it the idea of "making a parody of" something—Trans.]

5. Jacques Ruffie, *Le sexe et la mort* [*Sex and death*] (Paris: Odile Jacob, 1986), 270.

6. André Klarsfeld and Frédéric Revah, *The Biology of Death: Origins of Mortality*, trans. Lydia Brady (Ithaca: Cornell University Press, 2004), 70. The passage is from the conclusion of the chapter devoted to the issues examined and discussed in what follows.

7. Ruffie, *Le sexe et la mort*, 260.

8. See Hans-Georg Gadamer, *Truth and Method* (New York: Crossroad, 1975), 351–66. Heidegger has shown in his own way, in section 74 of *Being and Time*, that historicity, that is, the relation of a historical being to the tradition in which he is immersed by and from his birth, must be understood as a heritage of possibilities.

9. We know that an oral tradition has existed and still exists that sometimes has nothing to envy in the written tradition with regard to the capacity for preservation and the transmission of the past. The most striking example is given by the Vedic tradition, in which transmission has been exclusively oral for centuries: recitation constitutes the only mode of transmission. See Pierre-Sylvain Filliozat, *The Sanskrit Language: An Overview. History and Structure, Linguistic and Philosophical Representations, Uses and Users*, trans. T. K. Gopalan (Varanasi: Indica Books, 2000).

10. Plato, *Phaedrus* 275b.

11. This is the expression Husserl uses in "The Origin of Geometry." In the text, which was translated into French and preceded by a very long preface by Derrida, who found in it the source of his own reflection on writing, Husserl underlines the necessity for science and knowledge in general to pass through writing. See Jacques Derrida, *Edmund Husserl's "Origin of Geometry": An Introduction*, trans. John P. Leavey, Jr. (Lincoln: University of Nebraska Press, 1989).

12. See Gadamer, *Truth and Method*, 142–50.

13. Karl Marx, "Contribution to the Critique of Hegel's *Philosophy of Right*," in Marx, *Critique of Hegel's 'Philosophy of Right*,' trans. and ed. J. J. O'Malley (Cambridge: Cambridge University Press, 1970), 137.

14. See Auguste Comte, *Système de politique positive; ou, Traité de sociologie instituant la religion et l'humanité*, 4 vols. (Paris: L. Mathias, 1851–1854), available in English as *System of Positive Polity* (New York: B. Franklin, 1968).

15. René Char, "La parole en archipel" [The word as archipelago], in *Oeuvres* (Paris: Gallimard), 359. Cited by Christian

Doumet in "Une profonde statue en rien: Mort, gloire, et immortalité dans la poésie moderne" [A profound statue built of
nothing: Death, glory, and immortality in modern poetry], in *La
mort et l'immortalité: Encyclopédie des savoirs et des croyances*
[Death and immortality: The encyclopedia of knowledge and be-
lief], ed. Frédéric Lenoir and Jean-Philippe de Tonnac (Paris:
Bayard, 2004), 994. [Several morsels of Char's collection do appear in English, but not the poem from which this citation is
extracted—Trans.]

16. Jacques Derrida, *Of Grammatology*, trans. Gayatri Chakra-
vorty Spivak (Baltimore: Johns Hopkins University Press, 1974,
1998), 69.

17. In this regard, it is probably Maurice Merleau-Ponty, in
his *Phenomenology of Perception*, trans. Colin Smith (New York:
Routledge, 1962), who has contributed the most decisively to
showing the abyss separating the body as an object of biological
science from the experience we have "from the inside" of our
"own body."

18. David Le Breton, "Le corps insuffisant: La quête conte-
mporain d'immortalité" [The insufficient body: The contemporary quest for immortality], in *La mort et l'immortalité*, 1000.

19. See Merleau-Ponty, *Phenomenology of Perception*, 214–32.

20. Le Breton, "Le corps insuffisant," 1001.

21. See David Le Breton, *L'adieu au corps* (Paris: Métaillé,
1999).

22. This is the case of the astrophysicist Trinh Xuan Thuan,
evoked by Le Breton in "Le corps insuffisant," 1005, or of the
English physicist George Dyson, who was the first (in 1979) to
envision this idea seriously. (See Nicolas Prantzos, "Vers le zéro
absolu: Hypothèses sur la fin de l'univers" [Toward absolute zero:
Hypotheses about the end of the universe], in *La mort et l'immortalité*, 1587.)

23. See Martin Heidegger, *The Principle of Reason*, trans. Reg-
inald Lilly (Bloomington: Indiana University Press, 1991), 124.

24. See David Le Breton, *Conduites à risque: Des jeux de mort
au jeu de vivre* [Risky behaviors: From the stakes of death to the
game of life], (Paris: PUF, 2002).

25. G. W. F. Hegel, "Lord and Bondsman," in *Phenomenology of Spirit*, trans. A. V. Miller (Oxford: Oxford University Press, 1977), 111–18.

26. This is the title of an article by Michel Haar dedicated to Emmanuel Levinas in the *Cahier de L'Herne: Emmanuel Levinas* (Paris: L'Herne, 1991), 525–38.

27. Levinas's work itself testifies to this turning. He claims in *Totality and Infinity* that "atheism conditions a veritable relation with a true God " and that "the dimension of the divine opens forth from the human face" in such a way that "there can be no 'knowledge' of God separated from the relationship with men,." The conclusion thus imposes itself: God can show himself only through the face of the other, and "everything that cannot be reduced to an interhuman relation represents not the superior form but the forever primitive form of religion." Emmanuel Levinas, *Totality and Infinity*, trans. Alphonso Lingis (The Hague: Martinus Nijhoff, 1979), 77–79.

28. Hannah Arendt, *The Life of the Mind, Volume 1: Thinking* (New York: Harcourt, Brace, Jovanovic, 1978), 19.

29. See Guy Debord, *The Society of the Spectacle*, trans Donald Nicholson-Smith (New York: Zone Books, 1994).

30. Jean-Paul Sartre, *Being and Nothingness*, trans Hazel Barnes (New York: Washington Square Press, 1954), 321.

31. Ibid.

32. See "Letter on Humanism," trans. Frank A. Capuzzi in Martin Heidegger, *Pathmarks*, ed. William McNeill (Cambridge: Cambridge University Press, 1998), 242.

3. Accepting Death

1. See *Matthew* 26:36–46 and *Mark* 14:32–40.

2. See *1 Thessalonians* 5:2.

3. It is again Saint Paul who is at the origin of this doctrine, when he declares in *1 Corinthians* 3:19 that the "wisdom of the world is foolishness in God's eyes," with the term "world" characterizing the fallen being of humanity.

4. See Jean Delumeau, "L'art de bien mourir: Les *artes moriendi* de la Renaissance et les 'Pensez-y bien' du XVIIe siècle"

[The art of dying well: The *artes moriendi* of the Renaissance and the "Pensez-y bien" of the seventeenth century], in *La mort et l'immortalité: Encyclopédie des savoirs et des croyances* [Death and immortality: The encyclopedia of knowledge and belief], ed. Frédéric Lenoir and Jean-Philippe de Tonnac (Paris: Bayard, 2004), 211.

5. Ibid., 220.

6. Paul, *Romans* 4:18.

7. Paul, *1 Corinthians* 15:52–55.

8. Plato, *Phaedo* 67e. The verb *meletao* that Plato uses here means "to be concerned about," "to take care to," and "to make an effort," all at the same time [as well as "to care for," "to study or ponder," and "to be diligent"—Trans].

9. Ibid., 80e–81a.

10. Ibid., 64a.

11. Plato, *Phaedrus* 278c.

12. Blaise Pascal, *Pensées* (Lafuma edition, 612; Brunschvicg edition, 219).

13. See Michel de Montaigne, "That to Philosophize Is to Learn to Die," in Montaigne, *The Complete Essays of Montaigne*, trans. Donald M. Frame (Stanford: Stanford University Press, 1958), book 1, chapter 20, 56.

14. Michel de Montaigne, "Of Fear," in *The Complete Essays*, book 1, chapter 19, 55.

15. [The terms here appear to be a paraphrase of an argument in Michel de Montaigne, "Of Experience," in *The Complete Essays*, book 3, chapter 13, 815–57.—Trans.]

16. Montaigne, "That to Philosophize Is to Learn to Die," 66.

17. Ibid., 60.

18. Michel de Montaigne, "Of Practice, In *The Complete Essays*, book 2, chapter 6, 272. [Montaigne uses the verb *s'avoisiner*, which can mean to be neighbors or neighborly with, to live in the neighborhood with my neighbor, *mon voisin*, who is familiar to me because I see him, *je le vois*; one must thus learn to live nearby, to be neighbors with, death, which becomes more familiar to me when I learn to see it.—Trans.]

19. Montaigne, "That to Philosophize Is to Learn to Die," 65.

20. See in this regard Merleau-Ponty claiming in "Eye and Mind" that his is not "scientific thinking, a thinking which looks on from above, and thinks of the object in general," but a thought rooted in "a preliminary 'there is' which underlies it . . . the site, the soil of the sensible and opened world.." Maurice Merleau-Ponty, "Eye and Mind," trans. Carleton Dallery, in *The Primacy of Perception* (Evanston: Northwestern University Press, 1964), 160.

21. Spinoza, *Ethics*, part 4, prop. 67, in *A Spinoza Reader: The "Ethics" and Other Works*, ed. and trans. Edwin Curley (Princeton: Princeton University Press, 1994), 235.

22. Ibid., part 5, prop. 23, 256.

23. Ibid., part 5, prop. 23, schol, 256.

24. See Plato, *Theaetetus* 155d; *Phaedrus* 249a

25. See René Descartes, *Meditations on First Philosophy*, trans. Donald A. Cress (Indianapolis: Hackett, 1979), "Third Meditation," 30: "I clearly understand that there is more reality in an infinite substance than there is in a finite one. Thus the perception of the infinite somehow exists in me prior to the perception of the finite, that is, the perception of God exists prior to the perception of myself."

26. It is important to underline that the term *therapeia* first of all had the meaning in Greek of "concern," of "cultivation" and of solicitude with regard to the gods before acquiring the more determinate meaning of "care" in the properly medical sense of the term.

27. See Hans-Georg Gadamer, "The Experience of Death," in Gadamer, *The Enigma of Health,* trans. Jason Gaiger and Nicholas Walker (Stanford: Stanford University Press: 1996), 62, where he evokes the entry of the experience of death in "the technological business of industrial production."

28. This is what Aristotle claims in a passage in his *Physics* (book 2, 192b23–27) where, taking as an example the doctor who heals himself, he explains that it is not his status as doctor,

but rather his status as human that is the principle of his healing, with medical knowledge being able only to support and guide nature, not substitute for it.

29. This expression of an Anglo-Saxon origin implies that it is essentially a matter, by such care, of alleviating suffering in the terminal phase of life. We can prefer to it instead the term used in France, *accompaniment*, which designates the ensemble of relations with a sick person at the end of life. See René Schaerer, "La bonne mort: Naissance des soins palliatifs" [The good death: The birth of palliative care], in *La mort et l'immortalité*, 1113–28.

30. Heidegger calls this solicitude a "leap ahead," a kind of distancing in order to remove obstacles, precisely because it anticipates the capacity that the existing being has to accept its own destiny. See Martin Heidegger, *Being and Time*, trans. Joan Stambaugh (Albany: State University of New York Press, 1996), section 26, 115.

31. This formula is taken from Pindar's second *Pythian* ode, and in some way, Nietzsche makes this into his own maxim. See *Pythian* 2, ep. 3, line 72, "Be what you have learned you are," in *Pindar's Odes*, ed. and trans. Roy Arthur Swanson (New York: Bobbs-Merrill, 1974), 72.

32. See "On the Afterworldly," in Nietzsche, *Thus Spoke Zarathustra*, in *The Portable Nietzsche*, trans. and ed. Walter Kaufmann (New York: Viking, 1954), 142–43.

33. Martin Heidegger, "The Thing," trans. Albert Hofstadter in *Poetry, Language, Thought* (New York: Harper and Rowe, 1975), 179.

34. Ibid., 178: "The mortals are humans beings. They are called mortals because they can die. To die means to be capable of death as death."